Adult
MAD LIBS®

World's Greatest Word Game

TEST YOUR RELATIONSHIP IQ MAD LIBS

By Roger Price and Leonard Stern

PSS!
PRICE STERN SLOAN

ROADSIDE AMUSEMENTS
an imprint of
CHAMBERLAIN BROS.
Published by the Penguin Group
Price Stern Sloan, a division of Penguin Group for Young Readers.
Penguin Group (USA) Inc., 375 Hudson Street, New York, New York 10014, USA
Penguin Group (Canada), 10 Alcorn Avenue, Toronto, Ontario, Canada M4V 3B2
(a division of Pearson Penguin Canada Inc.)
Penguin Books Ltd, 80 Strand, London WC2R 0RL, England
Penguin Ireland, 25 St Stephen's Green, Dublin 2, Ireland (a division of Penguin Books Ltd)
Penguin Group (Australia), 250 Camberwell Road, Camberwell, Victoria 3124, Australia
(a division of Pearson Australia Group Pty Ltd)
Penguin Books India Pvt Ltd, 11 Community Centre, Panchsheel Park,
New Delhi–110 017, India
Penguin Group (NZ), Cnr Airborne and Rosedale Roads,
Albany, Auckland 1310, New Zealand (a division of Pearson New Zealand Ltd)
Penguin Books (South Africa) (Pty) Ltd, 24 Sturdee Avenue,
Rosebank, Johannesburg 2196, South Africa

Penguin Books Ltd, Registered Offices: 80 Strand, London WC2R 0RL, England

An application has been submitted to register this book with the Library of Congress.

ISBN 1-59609-151-7
2007 PRINTING

Printed in the United States of America

PSS! and *MAD LIBS* are registered trademarks of Penguin Group (USA) Inc.

MAD LIBS
INSTRUCTIONS

MAD LIBS® is a game for people who don't like games!
It can be played by one, two, three, four, or forty.

• RIDICULOUSLY SIMPLE DIRECTIONS

In this tablet you will find stories containing blank spaces where words are left out. One player, the **READER**, selects one of these stories. The **READER** does not tell anyone what the story is about. Instead, he/she asks the other players, the **WRITERS**, to give him/her words. These words are used to fill in the blank spaces in the story.

• TO PLAY

The **READER** asks each **WRITER** in turn to call out a word—an adjective or a noun or whatever the space calls for—and uses them to fill in the blank spaces in the story. The result is a **MAD LIBS®** game.

When the **READER** then reads the completed **MAD LIBS®** game to the other players, they will discover that they have written a story that is fantastic, screamingly funny, shocking, silly, crazy, or just plain dumb—depending upon which words each **WRITER** called out.

• EXAMPLE (*Before* and *After*)

"_____!" he said _____
 EXCLAMATION   ADVERB

as he jumped into his convertible _____ and
                                              NOUN

drove off with his _____ wife.
                          ADJECTIVE

"_____*Ouch*_____!" he said _____*stupidly*_____
 EXCLAMATION   ADVERB

as he jumped into his convertible _____*cat*_____ and
                                              NOUN

drove off with his _____*brave*_____ wife.
                          ADJECTIVE

MAD LIBS®
QUICK REVIEW

In case you have forgotten what adjectives, adverbs, nouns, and verbs are, here is a quick review:

An **ADJECTIVE** describes something or somebody. *Lumpy, soft, ugly, messy,* and *short* are adjectives.

An **ADVERB** tells how something is done. It modifies a verb and usually ends in "ly." *Modestly, stupidly, greedily,* and *carefully* are adverbs.

A **NOUN** is the name of a person, place, or thing. *Sidewalk, umbrella, bridle, bathtub,* and *nose* are nouns.

A **VERB** is an action word. *Run, pitch, jump,* and *swim* are verbs. Put the verbs in past tense if the directions say PAST TENSE. *Ran, pitched, jumped,* and *swam* are verbs in the past tense.

When we ask for **A PLACE**, we mean any sort of place: a country or city *(Spain, Cleveland)* or a room *(bathroom, kitchen).*

An **EXCLAMATION** or **SILLY WORD** is any sort of funny sound, gasp, grunt, or outcry, like *Wow!, Ouch!, Whomp!, Ick!,* and *Gadzooks!*

When we ask for specific words, like a **NUMBER**, a **COLOR**, an **ANIMAL**, or a **PART OF THE BODY**, we mean a word that is one of those things, like *seven, blue, horse,* or *head.*

When we ask for a **PLURAL**, it means more than one. For example, *cat* pluralized is *cats.*

MAD LIBS® is fun to play with friends, but you can also play it by yourself! To begin with, DO NOT look at the story on the page below. Fill in the blanks on this page with the words called for. Then, using the words you have selected, fill in the blank spaces in the story.

Now you've created your own hilarious MAD LIBS® game!

ARE YOU TRULY COMPATIBLE?

VERB _____

ADJECTIVE _____

ADJECTIVE _____

NOUN _____

ADJECTIVE _____

PLURAL NOUN _____

NOUN _____

VERB ENDING IN "ING" _____

VERB _____

ADJECTIVE _____

NOUN _____

ADJECTIVE _____

ADJECTIVE _____

TYPE OF LIQUID _____

VERB _____

ADJECTIVE _____

MAD LIBS
ARE YOU TRULY COMPATIBLE?

Sure, opposites _____, but you and your _____
                        VERB   ADJECTIVE

man still need to be compatible. Take this _____ quiz
                                                    ADJECTIVE

to see if he's the yin to your _____.
                                      NOUN

Which scenario best matches your _____ Friday night?
                                          ADJECTIVE

(a) He hangs out with his _____, while you stay home
                                PLURAL NOUN

and read a/an _____. Then, on Saturday, you spend all
                    NOUN

day _____ together.
        VERB ENDING IN "ING"

(b) You whine and ask him to _____ between you and
                                    VERB

his friends.

(c) You argue. He says you're _____ for wanting to stay
                                      ADJECTIVE

in your _____ all night and he pressures you into going
              NOUN

to a/an _____ event.
                ADJECTIVE

(d) You stay home. You rent a/an _____ romantic
                                          ADJECTIVE

comedy and pour yourself a glass of _____, while he
                                            TYPE OF LIQUID

plays _____-station 2 all night.
              VERB

Answer: (a) or (c) isn't too _____.
                                    ADJECTIVE

MAD LIBS® is fun to play with friends, but you can also play it by yourself! To begin with, DO NOT look at the story on the page below. Fill in the blanks on this page with the words called for. Then, using the words you have selected, fill in the blank spaces in the story.

Now you've created your own hilarious MAD LIBS® game!

IS HE REALLY COMMITTED?

ADJECTIVE _____

VERB _____

PLURAL NOUN _____

ADJECTIVE _____

NOUN _____

PART OF THE BODY _____

VERB _____

PLURAL NOUN _____

NOUN _____

EXCLAMATION _____

ADJECTIVE _____

NOUN _____

PLURAL NOUN _____

ADJECTIVE _____

VERB _____

MAD LIBS
IS HE REALLY COMMITTED?

Commitment makes some men feel pretty _____. If
                                          ADJECTIVE
they start to _____ intimacy, they turn into
                    VERB
_____. Take this _____ quiz to figure
   PLURAL NOUN   ADJECTIVE
out if he's in it for the long _____ . . . or if he has one
                                      NOUN
_____ out the door.
   PART OF THE BODY
When you ask him to _____ your parents, he:
                            VERB

(a) Claims he has front row_____ to the
                                      PLURAL NOUN
_____ game for that night.
      NOUN

(b) Says, "_____! Why?"
              EXCLAMATION

(c) Looks at you with _____ eyes and says it would be
                            ADJECTIVE
a/an _____ to meet them.
         NOUN

(d) Starts packing his _____.
                            PLURAL NOUN

Answer: This one doesn't count. Your parents are a little too

_____ to introduce him to, anyway, especially if you
      ADJECTIVE
don't want to _____ him off.
                    VERB

From TEST YOUR RELATIONSHIP IQ MAD LIBS® • Copyright © 2005 by Chamberlain Bros.,
a division of Penguin Group (USA), Inc., 375 Hudson Street, New York, New York 10014.

MAD LIBS® is fun to play with friends, but you can also play it by yourself! To begin with, DO NOT look at the story on the page below. Fill in the blanks on this page with the words called for. Then, using the words you have selected, fill in the blank spaces in the story.

Now you've created your own hilarious MAD LIBS® game!

HOW TO RAISE YOUR I.Q.: NUMBER 1

NUMBER _____

VERB _____

ADJECTIVE_____

ADJECTIVE_____

VERB _____

PART OF THE BODY (PLURAL) _____

PART OF THE BODY (PLURAL) _____

ADJECTIVE_____

ADVERB_____

ADJECTIVE_____

NOUN _____

PART OF THE BODY _____

SAME PART OF THE BODY_____

VERB _____

ADJECTIVE_____

MAD LIBS
HOW TO RAISE YOUR I.Q.: NUMBER 1

You haven't had a date in _____ months. Don't
NUMBER

_____ . You just need some _____
VERB   ADJECTIVE

pointers to raise your relationship I.Q.

• When arriving at a/an _____ party, be the first to
ADJECTIVE

_____ into the room. This way, all _____
VERB   PART OF THE BODY (PLURAL)

are on you.

• Be relaxed. Keep your _____ at your sides
PART OF THE BODY (PLURAL)

especially when you're speaking to a/an _____ guy.
ADJECTIVE

You don't want him to think you're _____ nervous.
ADVERB

• "Mirroring" is a/an _____ technique. While talking to that
ADJECTIVE

special _____ , you should note the position of his
NOUN

_____ , then rearrange your own _____
PART OF THE BODY   SAME PART OF THE BODY

in the same manner.

• When in doubt, _____ ! A/an _____ smile
VERB   ADJECTIVE

will always attract admirers.

From TEST YOUR RELATIONSHIP IQ MAD LIBS® • Copyright © 2005 by Chamberlain Bros.,
a division of Penguin Group (USA), Inc., 375 Hudson Street, New York, New York 10014.

MAD LIBS® is fun to play with friends, but you can also play it by yourself! To begin with, DO NOT look at the story on the page below. Fill in the blanks on this page with the words called for. Then, using the words you have selected, fill in the blank spaces in the story.

Now you've created your own hilarious MAD LIBS® game!

IS HE CHEATING ON YOU?

NOUN _____

PLURAL NOUN _____

ADJECTIVE_____

ADJECTIVE_____

NOUN _____

ARTICLE OF CLOTHING_____

TYPE OF FURNITURE _____

NOUN _____

NOUN _____

NOUN _____

MAD LIBS

IS HE CHEATING ON YOU?

Your sweetie has been a little distant lately, and you've been

wondering if he's a total _____ or a true blue fella.
NOUN

Answer true or false to the following _____ to see if
PLURAL NOUN

he's being faithful.

True or False

1) More than once he's cancelled a/an _____ date with
ADJECTIVE

you claiming a/an _____ emergency at the _____
ADJECTIVE ‎ NOUN

came up!

2) You find a pair of women's _____ under the
ARTICLE OF CLOTHING

_____—and they can't be yours, because you never
TYPE OF FURNITURE

wear any.

3) He says he's going to play a round of _____ with the
NOUN

guys, but when you follow him disguised as a/an _____,
NOUN

you see him at a poker _____ instead.
NOUN

If you answered True to (3), you might want to stop stalking the guy.

From TEST YOUR RELATIONSHIP IQ MAD LIBS® • Copyright © 2005 by Chamberlain Bros.,
a division of Penguin Group (USA), Inc., 375 Hudson Street, New York, New York 10014.

MAD LIBS® is fun to play with friends, but you can also play it by yourself! To begin with, DO NOT look at the story on the page below. Fill in the blanks on this page with the words called for. Then, using the words you have selected, fill in the blank spaces in the story.

Now you've created your own hilarious MAD LIBS® game!

IS HE YOUR SOUL MATE?

ADJECTIVE_____

PLURAL NOUN _____

VERB (PAST TENSE)_____

PART OF THE BODY (PLURAL) _____

NOUN _____

EXCLAMATION_____

NOUN _____

PART OF THE BODY_____

NOUN _____

ANIMAL _____

TYPE OF LIQUID _____

ANIMAL (PLURAL) _____

VERB ENDING IN "ING" _____

VERB _____

ADVERB_____

MAD LIBS
IS HE YOUR SOUL MATE?

If you believe in the _____ idea of soul
                                ADJECTIVE

_____, you'd better decide whether this romance is
   PLURAL NOUN

really written in the stars.

Which best describes how you _____ for the first time?
                                   VERB (PAST TENSE)

(a) When your _____ met across a crowded
                 PART OF THE BODY (PLURAL)

_____, he made his way over and whispered
           NOUN

"_____! You are one hot _____!" into
   EXCLAMATION   NOUN

your _____.
     PART OF THE BODY

(b) You met at a/an _____, where you both ordered
                         NOUN

_____ sandwiches with no crusts and a bottle of
     ANIMAL

_____ to go. Coincidence, or fate?
 TYPE OF LIQUID

(c) The leams of your _____ were intertwined when
                         ANIMAL (PLURAL)

you were_____ at a corner, and you've been inseperable
      VERB ENDING IN "ING"

ever since.

Answer: If you met your man in any of these situations,

_____ him— _____!
       VERB   ADVERB

MAD LIBS® is fun to play with friends, but you can also play it by yourself! To begin with, DO NOT look at the story on the page below. Fill in the blanks on this page with the words called for. Then, using the words you have selected, fill in the blank spaces in the story.

Now you've created your own hilarious MAD LIBS® game!

SHOULD YOU DUMP HIM?

NOUN _____

ADJECTIVE _____

VERB _____

NUMBER _____

NOUN _____

NUMBER _____

PLURAL NOUN _____

PLURAL NOUN _____

PART OF THE BODY _____

ADJECTIVE _____

NOUN _____

VERB _____

MAD LIBS
SHOULD YOU DUMP HIM?

We know being single can be awful, but there comes a time when

you have to throw in the _____ on a/an _____
NOUN   ADJECTIVE

relationship. Take this quiz to figure out if you need to

_____ this guy and/or move on.
VERB

When you think of your boyfriend you:

(a) Remember the _____ dollars he owes you from the
NUMBER

time he desperately needed to fix his _____. (This
NOUN

was _____ months ago.)
NUMBER

(b) Think of his hot best friend, the one who always wears tight

_____ to show off his _____.
PLURAL NOUN   PLURAL NOUN

(c) Cry. Your _____ was upset last night and he didn't
PART OF THE BODY

come by like he promised.

(d) Feel all warm and _____ when picturing him on your
ADJECTIVE

first date, but then you remember the icky _____ on his neck.
NOUN

Answer: If you chose any of the above you need to _____
VERB

this guy and be a single chick again for awhile.

From TEST YOUR RELATIONSHIP IQ MAD LIBS® • Copyright © 2005 by Chamberlain Bros.,
a division of Penguin Group (USA), Inc., 375 Hudson Street, New York, New York 10014.

MAD LIBS® is fun to play with friends, but you can also play it by yourself! To begin with, DO NOT look at the story on the page below. Fill in the blanks on this page with the words called for. Then, using the words you have selected, fill in the blank spaces in the story.

Now you've created your own hilarious MAD LIBS® game!

IS HE PULLING AWAY?

ADJECTIVE _____

VERB ENDING IN "ING" _____

ADJECTIVE _____

PLURAL NOUN _____

ADJECTIVE _____

NOUN _____

VERB _____

ADJECTIVE _____

COLOR _____

TYPE OF LIQUID _____

PART OF THE BODY (PLURAL) _____

VERB ENDING IN "ING" _____

PART OF THE BODY _____

LANGUAGE _____

VERB _____

ADVERB _____

MAD LIBS®
IS HE PULLING AWAY?

As much as we'd like to deny it, _____ love doesn't

ADJECTIVE

always last forever. Do you feel him _____ interest in

VERB ENDING IN "ING"

you? Take this _____ quiz to find out he's ready to call

ADJECTIVE

it _____ . . . or if he's just in a/an _____ mood.

PLURAL NOUN · ADJECTIVE

You suggest planning a trip to a foreign _____. He:

NOUN

(a) Starts to squirm and _____ in his seat, saying how

VERB

his schedule tends to be really_____ that time of year.

ADJECTIVE

(b) Asks if you want red or _____ _____

COLOR · TYPE OF LIQUID

with your pasta.

(c) Wrings his _____, claiming he's afraid of

PART OF THE BODY (PLURAL)

_____. When the plane reaches high altitudes

VERB ENDING IN "ING"

his _____ bleeds.

PART OF THE BODY

(d) Suggests you start taking _____ next week so that

LANGUAGE

you can _____ with the locals.

VERB

Answer: If (d) is his reply, book your flight_____, if

ADVERB

not sooner.

MAD LIBS® is fun to play with friends, but you can also play it by yourself! To begin with, DO NOT look at the story on the page below. Fill in the blanks on this page with the words called for. Then, using the words you have selected, fill in the blank spaces in the story.

Now you've created your own hilarious MAD LIBS® game!

HOW TO RAISE YOUR I.Q.: NUMBER 2

NOUN _____

VERB ENDING IN "ING" _____

NOUN _____

PLURAL NOUN _____

NOUN _____

ADJECTIVE_____

ARTICLE OF CLOTHING_____

PLURAL NOUN _____

NOUN _____

NOUN _____

A PLACE _____

PLURAL NOUN _____

VERB _____

PLURAL NOUN _____

NOUN _____

NOUN _____

NOUN _____

You've mastered the art of _____ Language, but you're

NOUN

still _____ at home on a Saturday night, watching

VERB ENDING IN "ING"

T.V., eating junk _____ and wondering why you can't

NOUN

meet a guy like that hunk on *Desperate* _____.

PLURAL NOUN

Well, sister, put down that _____, and put on your

NOUN

_____ _____. You're going out!

ADJECTIVE   ARTICLE OF CLOTHING

• Scan the internet to find groups who are dedicated to the same

_____ you are.

PLURAL NOUN

• If you have ever wanted to learn how to _____, how

NOUN

about taking a beginner's _____ at the local _____.

NOUN   A PLACE

• Ask your _____ about groups or events they are

PLURAL NOUN

involved in then ask to _____ along.

VERB

• Organize a monthly "_____ Night Out" with all the

PLURAL NOUN

ladies listed in your personal _____.

NOUN

Remember—nobody ever found the _____ of their

NOUN

dreams by staying at home night after _____!

NOUN

From TEST YOUR RELATIONSHIP IQ MAD LIBS® • Copyright © 2005 by Chamberlain Bros.,
a division of Penguin Group (USA), Inc., 375 Hudson Street, New York, New York 10014.

MAD LIBS® is fun to play with friends, but you can also play it by yourself! To begin with, DO NOT look at the story on the page below. Fill in the blanks on this page with the words called for. Then, using the words you have selected, fill in the blank spaces in the story.

Now you've created your own hilarious MAD LIBS® game!

DOES HE FLIRT TOO MUCH?

ADJECTIVE _____

VERB _____

ADJECTIVE _____

NOUN _____

A PLACE _____

ADJECTIVE _____

PART OF THE BODY _____

ADJECTIVE _____

PART OF THE BODY _____

ADJECTIVE _____

ADJECTIVE _____

NUMBER _____

TYPE OF LIQUID _____

VERB _____

ADJECTIVE _____

MAD LIBS
DOES HE FLIRT TOO MUCH?

Flirting is _____, but does he _____
$\qquad$ ADJECTIVE $\qquad\qquad\qquad$ VERB

over the line? Take this _____ quiz to see if he's just
$\qquad\qquad$ ADJECTIVE

having fun or making a/an _____ out of you.
$\qquad\qquad$ NOUN

When you go out together to a/an _____, he:
$\qquad\qquad$ A PLACE

(a) Scopes the room out for _____ babes.
$\qquad\qquad$ ADJECTIVE

(b) Takes you by the _____ leads you to a/an
$\qquad\qquad$ PART OF THE BODY

_____ table.
ADJECTIVE

(c) Makes lingering _____ contact with anyone
$\qquad\qquad$ PART OF THE BODY

wearing a/an _____ skirt.
$\qquad\qquad$ ADJECTIVE

(d) Gets distracted by _____ women for at least
$\qquad\qquad$ ADJECTIVE

_____ minutes every time he goes to the bar to get
NUMBER

more _____.
$\qquad$ TYPE OF LIQUID

Answer: Who cares? If it's (a), (b), (c) or (d), it stinks! Why don't you

go _____ with that _____ blonde guy
$\qquad$ VERB $\qquad\qquad\qquad$ ADJECTIVE

over there who's been flirting with you the entire evening?

From TEST YOUR RELATIONSHIP IQ MAD LIBS® • Copyright © 2005 by Chamberlain Bros.,
a division of Penguin Group (USA), Inc., 375 Hudson Street, New York, New York 10014.

MAD LIBS® is fun to play with friends, but you can also play it by yourself! To begin with, DO NOT look at the story on the page below. Fill in the blanks on this page with the words called for. Then, using the words you have selected, fill in the blank spaces in the story.

Now you've created your own hilarious MAD LIBS® game!

ARE YOU READY TO MOVE IN TOGETHER?

ADJECTIVE_____

ADJECTIVE_____

PLURAL NOUN _____

PLURAL NOUN _____

ADJECTIVE_____

NOUN _____

ADJECTIVE _____

NUMBER _____

PART OF THE BODY _____

NOUN _____

NOUN _____

VERB ENDING IN "ING" _____

PLURAL NOUN _____

ADVERB_____

NUMBER _____

ADJECTIVE_____

MAD LIBS®
ARE YOU READY TO MOVE IN TOGETHER?

You've been together for months. You practically live together already,

but is it time to make the _____ move? Take this
                              ADJECTIVE

_____ quiz to help you decide whether you should start
ADJECTIVE

packing your _____ . . . or leave your _____
             PLURAL NOUN   PLURAL NOUN

where they are.

Pick which of these _____ scenarios best applies to
                    ADJECTIVE

you and your _____ .
             NOUN

(a) You hate being _____ , even for _____ seconds.
                   ADJECTIVE   NUMBER

(b) He drives you out of your _____ when he forgets
                             PART OF THE BODY

to put down the toilet _____ .
                       NOUN

(c) He always leaves the _____ door open while
                         NOUN

_____ .
VERB ENDING IN "ING"

(d) You discover a stash of _____ in his closet, which
                            PLURAL NOUN

_____ freaks you out.
ADVERB

Answer: Let's face it, the _____ dollars you'll save on
                           NUMBER

rent will be worth the _____ gamble on the relationship.
                       ADJECTIVE

From TEST YOUR RELATIONSHIP IQ MAD LIBS® • Copyright © 2005 by Chamberlain Bros.,
a division of Penguin Group (USA), Inc., 375 Hudson Street, New York, New York 10014.

MAD LIBS® is fun to play with friends, but you can also play it by yourself! To begin with, DO NOT look at the story on the page below. Fill in the blanks on this page with the words called for. Then, using the words you have selected, fill in the blank spaces in the story.

Now you've created your own hilarious MAD LIBS® game!

IS HE TOO SELFISH?

VERB _____

ADJECTIVE _____

ADVERB _____

ADJECTIVE _____

ADVERB _____

ADJECTIVE _____

SILLY WORD _____

PART OF THE BODY _____

NUMBER _____

NOUN _____

NOUN _____

ADVERB _____

NUMBER _____

ADJECTIVE _____

PLURAL NOUN _____

PLURAL NOUN _____

NOUN _____

MAD LIBS®
IS HE TOO SELFISH?

Naturally, people have to _____ for themselves, but is
                              VERB

your _____ guy _____ selfish? Take this
        ADJECTIVE   ADVERB

_____ quiz to figure out if he's _____ a good
   ADJECTIVE   ADVERB

guy . . . or just a whiny _____ _____.
                              ADJECTIVE   SILLY WORD

It's your anniversary and he:

(a) Rubs your _____ for _____ minutes
                PART OF THE BODY   NUMBER

but complains the whole time.

b) Asks if you can postpone your anniversary _____
                                                    NOUN

until tomorrow night. The Super _____ is on tonight.
                                      NOUN

c) _____ makes reservations at your favorite
      ADVERB

restaurant—for you and _____ of his _____ friends.
                          NUMBER   ADJECTIVE

d) Forgets important _____—he's never been very
                          PLURAL NOUN

good about remembering _____.
                            PLURAL NOUN

Answer: He's a man—of course he's going to be a selfish

_____.
   NOUN

From TEST YOUR RELATIONSHIP IQ MAD LIBS® • Copyright © 2005 by Chamberlain Bros.,
a division of Penguin Group (USA), Inc., 375 Hudson Street, New York, New York 10014.

MAD LIBS® is fun to play with friends, but you can also play it by yourself! To begin with, DO NOT look at the story on the page below. Fill in the blanks on this page with the words called for. Then, using the words you have selected, fill in the blank spaces in the story.

Now you've created your own hilarious MAD LIBS® game!

ARE YOU TOO DEMANDING?

PLURAL NOUN _____

PLURAL NOUN _____

ADJECTIVE_____

ADJECTIVE_____

ADJECTIVE_____

ROOM _____

VERB _____

NUMBER _____

ADJECTIVE_____

PART OF THE BODY (PLURAL) _____

NOUN _____

NOUN _____

NUMBER _____

ADJECTIVE_____

MAD LIBS®
ARE YOU TOO DEMANDING?

Women certainly know the many _____ to get what
                                    PLURAL NOUN

they want, but are we too demanding of our _____? Take
                                              PLURAL NOUN

this _____ quiz to figure out whether you're just a/an
        ADJECTIVE

_____ gal or if you need to learn to a little more flexible.
   ADJECTIVE

Which best describes what happens after a/an _____
                                                ADJECTIVE

argument?

(a) You go into the _____, slam the door, and wait for
                          ROOM

him to _____.
          VERB

(b) He spends _____ hours screaming and telling you
                    NUMBER

that you are _____.
                ADJECTIVE

(c) You fall into each other's _____ and you lead
                                 PART OF THE BODY (PLURAL)

him to the _____ immediately.
                NOUN

(d) You give him the silent _____ for _____ days
                              NOUN   NUMBER

before forgiving him.

Answer: Hopefully you picked (c)—you'll get _____
                                                ADJECTIVE

evening out of it!

From TEST YOUR RELATIONSHIP IQ MAD LIBS® • Copyright © 2005 by Chamberlain Bros.,
a division of Penguin Group (USA), Inc., 375 Hudson Street, New York, New York 10014.

MAD LIBS® is fun to play with friends, but you can also play it by yourself! To begin with, DO NOT look at the story on the page below. Fill in the blanks on this page with the words called for. Then, using the words you have selected, fill in the blank spaces in the story.

Now you've created your own hilarious MAD LIBS® game!

IS IT REALLY OVER

PLURAL NOUN _____

NOUN _____

NUMBER _____

EXCLAMATION _____

NOUN _____

PLURAL NOUN _____

A HOLIDAY _____

PLURAL NOUN _____

NOUN _____

NOUN _____

PERSON IN ROOM (FEMALE) _____

MAD LIBS
IS IT REALLY OVER

You were arguing a lot until he announced it was over. But you're

wondering if it really is. Answer True or False to the following

_____ and find out if there's hope or if you should
PLURAL NOUN

just get on with your _____.
NOUN

True or False

1) He'll call you _____ times a day, just to say "_____!"
NUMBER   EXCLAMATION

2) He keeps stopping by your _____ to ask for his
NOUN

_____ back.
PLURAL NOUN

3) His mother calls you inviting you to _____ _____
A HOLIDAY   PLURAL NOUN

and tells you that he is still thinks the _____ of you.
NOUN

4) You saw him driving around in a/an _____ that you
NOUN

think belongs to _____.
PERSON IN ROOM (FEMALE)

If you answered "True" to number 4, you may as well face it. It's over.

From TEST YOUR RELATIONSHIP IQ MAD LIBS® • Copyright © 2005 by Chamberlain Bros.,
a division of Penguin Group (USA), Inc., 375 Hudson Street, New York, New York 10014.

MAD LIBS® is fun to play with friends, but you can also play it by yourself! To begin with, DO NOT look at the story on the page below. Fill in the blanks on this page with the words called for. Then, using the words you have selected, fill in the blank spaces in the story.

Now you've created your own hilarious MAD LIBS® game!

IS HE JUST A JERK?

NOUN _____

NOUN _____

VERB _____

ADJECTIVE _____

ADJECTIVE _____

ADJECTIVE _____

ADJECTIVE _____

ADVERB _____

SILLY WORD _____

VERB _____

VERB _____

EXCLAMATION _____

NOUN _____

ADJECTIVE _____

NOUN _____

NOUN _____

MAD LIBS®
IS HE JUST A JERK?

Sure, he can be an annoying _____ to your friends
                                    NOUN

and sometimes, unexplainably loses his _____, but is he
                                                NOUN

really just a jerk? _____ this quiz to figure out if your
                            VERB

man is a nice guy or a/an _____ jerk.
                                ADJECTIVE

His best friend just went through a/an _____
                                                ADJECTIVE

breakup. He responds to the news by saying:

(a) "Are you _____? She was a/an _____!"
                ADJECTIVE   ADJECTIVE

(b) "I _____ thought she was a little _____
            ADVERB   SILLY WORD

in the head."

(c) "Man, I'm so thrilled I can hardly _____. Now you can
                                                VERB

hang out with me and we can double _____ like old times."
                                            VERB

(d) "_____! She wasn't your _____. She was as
        EXCLAMATION   NOUN

_____ as a/an _____ anyway!"
        ADJECTIVE   NOUN

Answer: If the answer is (a) and (b), he's a first class jerk, but (c) and

(d) say he's a _____ who cares.
                    NOUN

From TEST YOUR RELATIONSHIP IQ MAD LIBS® • Copyright © 2005 by Chamberlain Bros.,
a division of Penguin Group (USA), Inc., 375 Hudson Street, New York, New York 10014.

MAD LIBS® is fun to play with friends, but you can also play it by yourself! To begin with, DO NOT look at the story on the page below. Fill in the blanks on this page with the words called for. Then, using the words you have selected, fill in the blank spaces in the story.

Now you've created your own hilarious MAD LIBS® game!

ARE YOU STILL HUNG UP ON HIM?

NUMBER _____

PART OF THE BODY _____

VERB _____

ADJECTIVE _____

OCCUPATION _____

ADJECTIVE _____

ARTICLE OF CLOTHING _____

VERB ENDING IN "ING" _____

NOUN _____

NOUN _____

ADJECTIVE _____

NOUN _____

NOUN _____

NUMBER _____

NOUN _____

NOUN _____

MAD LIBS®
ARE YOU STILL HUNG UP ON HIM?

OK, it's been _____ months since the breakup,
NUMBER

but does your _____ still feel freshly broken?
PART OF THE BODY

_____ this quiz to figure out if you're just feeling
VERB

_____ or are in need of seeing a/an _____.
ADJECTIVE   OCCUPATION

Have you been:

(a) Sleeping in his _____ old _____
ADJECTIVE   ARTICLE OF CLOTHING

every night?

(b) _____ every time you pass the _____
VERB ENDING IN "ING"   NOUN

where you went on your first _____?
NOUN

(c) Setting up a/an _____ shrine to him in your one
ADJECTIVE

room _____?
NOUN

(d) Stopping by his _____ where he works _____
NOUN   NUMBER

times a day to beg him for a second _____?
NOUN

Answer: If you picked (c) or (d), please see a licensed _____
NOUN

immediately.

From TEST YOUR RELATIONSHIP IQ MAD LIBS® • Copyright © 2005 by Chamberlain Bros.,
a division of Penguin Group (USA), Inc., 375 Hudson Street, New York, New York 10014.

MAD LIBS® is fun to play with friends, but you can also play it by yourself! To begin with, DO NOT look at the story on the page below. Fill in the blanks on this page with the words called for. Then, using the words you have selected, fill in the blank spaces in the story.

Now you've created your own hilarious MAD LIBS® game!

IS HE ROMANTIC?

PART OF THE BODY _____

ADJECTIVE _____

ADJECTIVE _____

NOUN _____

NOUN _____

ADJECTIVE _____

ADJECTIVE _____

PART OF THE BODY (PLURAL) _____

NOUN _____

ADJECTIVE _____

VERB _____

ADVERB _____

NOUN _____

ADJECTIVE _____

ADJECTIVE _____

ADJECTIVE _____

MAD LIBS®
IS HE ROMANTIC?

Sure, he makes your _____ flutter, but does he
<u>PART OF THE BODY</u>

qualify as a/an _____ romantic? Take this _____
<u>ADJECTIVE</u> <u>ADJECTIVE</u>

quiz to see if he is truly a/an _____ or if he is just like
<u>NOUN</u>

every other _____ you've dated.
<u>NOUN</u>

When you return from a/an _____ business trip and
<u>ADJECTIVE</u>

you're exhausted, does your man ...

(a) Pick you up at the airport with a/an _____ smile on
<u>ADJECTIVE</u>

his face and a bouquet of roses in his _____.
<u>PART OF THE BODY (PLURAL)</u>

(b) Turn down the volume of the _____ on TV briefly for
<u>NOUN</u>

a/an _____"hi" when you _____ through the door.
<u>ADJECTIVE</u> <u>VERB</u>

(c) Act _____ surprised to learn that you've been away.
<u>ADVERB</u>

(d) Expect you to immediately start cooking _____ for him?
<u>NOUN</u>

Answer: (a) makes him a/an _____ romantic at heart.
<u>ADJECTIVE</u>

If you picked (b), (c), or (d), you have a/an _____
<u>ADJECTIVE</u>

apple. The sooner you dump this _____ loser the better.
<u>ADJECTIVE</u>

From TEST YOUR RELATIONSHIP IQ MAD LIBS® • Copyright © 2005 by Chamberlain Bros.,
a division of Penguin Group (USA), Inc., 375 Hudson Street, New York, New York 10014.

MAD LIBS® is fun to play with friends, but you can also play it by yourself! To begin with, DO NOT look at the story on the page below. Fill in the blanks on this page with the words called for. Then, using the words you have selected, fill in the blank spaces in the story.

Now you've created your own hilarious MAD LIBS® game!

IS HE MR. RIGHT?

NOUN _____

ADJECTIVE_____

NOUN _____

ADJECTIVE_____

NOUN _____

NUMBER _____

ADJECTIVE_____

PLURAL NOUN _____

VERB _____

PART OF THE BODY (PLURAL) _____

NOUN _____

ADJECTIVE_____

ADJECTIVE_____

MAD LIBS

IS HE MR. RIGHT?

He might be the _____ of your life, but you're not sure yet.
                      NOUN

Let this _____ test help you decide if you should go
              ADJECTIVE

shopping for a diamond _____ or stop wasting your
                                    NOUN

_____ time.
    ADJECTIVE

Which of the following describes your relationship?

(a) When you call him to make plans, he says "whatever you want,

_____," then argues about it later.
      NOUN

(b) You both want a/an _____-bedroom house in a/an
                                   NUMBER

_____ neighborhood in the suburbs and are hoping
        ADJECTIVE

to have children and many _____.
                                   PLURAL NOUN

(c) He's noncritical. He adores how you always _____
                                                            VERB

with your _____, which most people find annoying.
            PART OF THE BODY (PLURAL)

(d) Your first name and his last _____ make a/an
                                           NOUN

_____ combination. Right?
        ADJECTIVE

Answer: If you checked (a), you might want to start looking for a/an

_____ guy.
        ADJECTIVE

From TEST YOUR RELATIONSHIP IQ MAD LIBS® • Copyright © 2005 by Chamberlain Bros.,
a division of Penguin Group (USA), Inc., 375 Hudson Street, New York, New York 10014.

MAD LIBS® is fun to play with friends, but you can also play it by yourself! To begin with, DO NOT look at the story on the page below. Fill in the blanks on this page with the words called for. Then, using the words you have selected, fill in the blank spaces in the story.

Now you've created your own hilarious MAD LIBS® game!

IT'S NOT YOU, IT'S ME . . .

ADJECTIVE_____

PLURAL NOUN _____

ADJECTIVE_____

NOUN _____

EXCLAMATION_____

ADJECTIVE_____

NOUN _____

PLURAL NOUN _____

PLURAL NOUN _____

TYPE OF EVENT _____

VERB (PAST TENSE)_____

VERB ENDING IN "ING" _____

NOUN _____

MAD LIBS®

IT'S NOT YOU, IT'S ME . . .

We've all heard it one time or another—the _____
ADJECTIVE

breakup line, "It's not you, it's me." But could it be you? Answer True

or False to the following _____ and find out.
PLURAL NOUN

True or False

1) Whenever he took you to a/an _____ restaurant and
ADJECTIVE

the waiter brought the _____ he would say
NOUN

"_____! You have _____ taste."
EXCLAMATION   ADJECTIVE

2) He says he'll go to your company's _____ party, but
NOUN

when the day arrives, he doesn't show because the _____
PLURAL NOUN

versus the _____ is on ESPN.
PLURAL NOUN

3) He didn't bother to show up at your surprise _____
TYPE OF EVENT

and your whole family was fit to be _____.
VERB (PAST TENSE)

I think I've heard enough. If you answered True to any of these, he's

not _____—it really isn't you, it's _____!
VERB ENDING IN "ING"   NOUN

Now isn't that a relief?

MAD LIBS® is fun to play with friends, but you can also play it by yourself! To begin with, DO NOT look at the story on the page below. Fill in the blanks on this page with the words called for. Then, using the words you have selected, fill in the blank spaces in the story.

Now you've created your own hilarious MAD LIBS® game!

HOW TO RAISE YOUR I.Q.: NUMBER 3

NOUN _____

VERB _____

ADJECTIVE_____

NOUN _____

GEOGRAPHIC LOCATION _____

NOUN _____

GEOGRAPHIC LOCATION _____

GEOGRAPHIC LOCATION _____

PLURAL NOUN _____

NOUN _____

NOUN _____

ADJECTIVE_____

NOUN _____

NOUN _____

VERB ENDING IN "ING" _____

ADJECTIVE_____

MAD LIBS
HOW TO RAISE YOUR I.Q.: NUMBER 3

You've gone over your Body Language notes, you've been taking

_____ classes and you've even learned how to
NOUN

_____ the Tango, but you're still not in a/an _____
VERB   ADJECTIVE

relationship. Maybe the problem is a little more complex than we

first thought. Here are some ways to deal with the _____:
NOUN

• Go to your local _____. Browse the Self-help section
GEOGRAPHIC LOCATION

for a/an _____ that addresses your particular issue.
NOUN

• Best-sellers like *Men are from* _____, *Women are*
GEOGRAPHIC LOCATION

from _____ have helped numerous people find
GEOGRAPHIC LOCATION

happiness in their _____.
PLURAL NOUN

• Make an appointment with a professional _____.
NOUN

Sometimes there is something in your _____ that is
NOUN

keeping you from finding a/an_____love.
ADJECTIVE

• Call your local _____ and ask if you can meet with
NOUN

an ordained _____. Sometimes just _____
NOUN   VERB ENDING IN "ING"

with a/an _____ person can help.
ADJECTIVE

MAD LIBS® is fun to play with friends, but you can also play it by yourself! To begin with, DO NOT look at the story on the page below. Fill in the blanks on this page with the words called for. Then, using the words you have selected, fill in the blank spaces in the story.

Now you've created your own hilarious MAD LIBS® game!

OFFICE ROMANCE

ADJECTIVE _____

ADJECTIVE _____

NOUN _____

ADJECTIVE _____

ADJECTIVE _____

NOUN _____

PLURAL NOUN _____

VERB ENDING IN "ING" _____

NOUN _____

NOUN _____

MAD LIBS®
OFFICE ROMANCE

There is a new guy in the office who you think has real potential.

And he's been acting really _____ around you lately.
  ADJECTIVE

Answer True or False to the following questions and find out if

something _____ could come out of this.
  ADJECTIVE

True or False

1) He brings you _____ danish every morning just
  NOUN

because he knows you like them.

2) He calls you into his office on _____ pretexts and
  ADJECTIVE

then will ask you _____ questions about your personal
  ADJECTIVE

_____.
  NOUN

3) He's invited you out for dinner and _____ after work.
  PLURAL NOUN

And he insists on _____ the check!
  VERB ENDING IN "ING"

If you answered true to any of these questions why are you taking a

test? You need to pick up the _____, call him into your
  NOUN

_____ and conduct some personal business.
  NOUN

From TEST YOUR RELATIONSHIP IQ MAD LIBS® • Copyright © 2005 by Chamberlain Bros.,
a division of Penguin Group (USA), Inc., 375 Hudson Street, New York, New York 10014.

MAD LIBS® is fun to play with friends, but you can also play it by yourself! To begin with, DO NOT look at the story on the page below. Fill in the blanks on this page with the words called for. Then, using the words you have selected, fill in the blank spaces in the story.

Now you've created your own hilarious MAD LIBS® game!

SHOULD YOU TAKE HIM BACK?

ADJECTIVE _____

NUMBER _____

ADJECTIVE _____

VERB (PAST TENSE) _____

ADJECTIVE _____

NOUN _____

VERB ENDING IN "ING" _____

TYPE OF FURNITURE _____

VERB ENDING IN "ING" _____

PART OF THE BODY _____

ADJECTIVE _____

ADVERB _____

VERB (PAST TENSE) _____

ADJECTIVE _____

ADJECTIVE _____

TYPE OF FOOD _____

TYPE OF FOOD _____

PART OF THE BODY _____

ADJECTIVE _____

MAD LIBS®
SHOULD YOU TAKE HIM BACK?

You had a/an _____ breakup _____
ADJECTIVE   NUMBER

years ago, but now he's back, looking as _____ as ever
ADJECTIVE

and claiming that he has _____ a lot. Take this
VERB (PAST TENSE)

_____ quiz to help you decide whether you should
ADJECTIVE

give him another _____ . . . or send him _____.
NOUN   VERB ENDING IN "ING"

You're sitting across the _____ from him. What's
TYPE OF FURNITURE

_____ through your mind?
VERB ENDING IN "ING"

(a) Does he still pick his _____?
PART OF THE BODY

(b) All of the _____ fights you used to have, and the
ADJECTIVE

last one where you _____ broke up.
ADVERB

(c) Amazement at how you ever could have _____
VERB (PAST TENSE)

this _____ guy.
ADJECTIVE

(d) The sparks are _____! Should you serve
ADJECTIVE

_____ or _____ at the wedding?
TYPE OF FOOD   TYPE OF FOOD

Answer: Let your _____ lead you to the _____
PART OF THE BODY   ADJECTIVE

decision.

From TEST YOUR RELATIONSHIP IQ MAD LIBS® • Copyright © 2005 by Chamberlain Bros.,
a division of Penguin Group (USA), Inc., 375 Hudson Street, New York, New York 10014.

Adult MAD LIBS®

World's Greatest Word Game
Roger Price and Leonard Stern

Look for these other fun Adult Mad Libs® titles at a bookseller near you!

ADVICE FOR THE LOVELORN

KEEPERS AND LOSERS

TEST YOUR RELATIONSHIP I.Q.

PARTY GIRL

BACHELORETTE BASH

DYSFUNCTIONAL FAMILY THERAPY

MAMA'S GOT A BRAND-NEW (DIAPER) BAG

WHO MOVED MY CUBICLE?